COUNTDOWN TO DISASTER
THE WORLD IN DANGER!

DAVID BURNIE

OXFORD
UNIVERSITY PRESS

OXFORD
UNIVERSITY PRESS

Great Clarendon Street, Oxford OX2 6DP

Oxford University Press is a department of the University of Oxford.
It furthers the University's objective of excellence in research,
scholarship, and education by publishing worldwide in

Oxford   New York

Auckland   Cape Town   Dar es Salaam   Hong Kong   Karachi
Kuala Lumpur   Madrid   Melbourne   Mexico City   Nairobi
New Delhi   Shanghai   Taipei   Toronto

With offices in

Argentina   Austria   Brazil   Chile   Czech Republic   France   Greece
Guatemala   Hungary   Italy   Japan   Poland   Portugal   Singapore
South Korea   Switzerland   Thailand   Turkey   Ukraine   Vietnam

Oxford is a registered trade mark of Oxford University Press
in the UK and in certain other countries

British Library Cataloguing in Publication Data

Data available

ISBN: 9780199117147

10 9 8 7 6 5 4 3 2 1

Originated by Oxford University Press
Created by Toucan Books Ltd

Printed in China

Contents

Introduction

MOST PEOPLE LIKE A GOOD SCARE, which is why disaster stories make gripping films. But this book isn't about imaginary disasters: it's about ones that can happen in real life. Even with modern technology, many of them still strike without warning, and once they have happened, their after-effects can last for months or even years.

Natural disasters happen on many different scales. Tornadoes are some of the smallest, but that doesn't stop them being deadly. These incredibly violent storms strike with the sharpness of a knife, sometimes destroying houses on one side of a street, while leaving others almost untouched. At the other extreme, the world's biggest disasters can affect many countries at once, leaving a trail of destruction hundreds of kilometres wide. In recent years, the worst example of this was the Indian Ocean tsunami, which struck in 2004. It affected countries all around the Indian Ocean in the space of a

The DEADLIEST natural disaster EVER was the *Yellow River Flood* in 1931. At least 2 million PEOPLE DIED

few hours. By the time it was over, more than 200,000 people had died, and many more had lost their homes.

Fortunately, disasters this big are rare, and your risk of getting caught up in any natural disaster is extremely small. But some disasters are so enormous that they leave no hiding place. They include collisions with giant objects from space – something that could happen in your lifetime, but almost certainly will not. They also include global warming, a slow-motion disaster that is happening right now. Unlike all the other disasters in this book, global warming is something we have helped to start. It's also something that we can all help to stop – before it is too late.

DAVID BURNIE

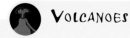

Volcanoes

No one knows how many volcanoes there are on Earth, because some of them are hidden far away on the deep seabed. However, on land there is no mistaking a volcano when it suddenly erupts. Millions of tonnes of ash and steam are blasted into the air, while rivers of lava often pour down a volcano's sides. From a distance, it's one of the most stunning sights in nature, but it can be terrifying when witnessed up close. Volcanoes sometimes give signs that they are about to explode, but often, an eruption literally comes out of the blue.

A truck speeds for safety before a huge cloud of ash, during the eruption of Mount Pinatubo in the Philippines in 1991. The ash fell like snow and reached as far as Singapore, over 2,000km away.

Time bombs

VOLCANOES MAKE DANGEROUS NEIGHBOURS, because it is impossible to know exactly what they will do next. Some are completely extinct. A few – like Stromboli off the coast of Italy – are active all the time. But the most deadly volcanoes are dormant ones. Like gigantic time bombs, they can stay silent for centuries or even thousands of years, before suddenly exploding back into life.

SUDDEN AWAKENING

For hundreds of years, El Chichón in Mexico was thought to be extinct. However, the volcano was just dormant, and in 1982 its long sleep came to an end. Three colossal explosions, just days apart, shook the volcano, killing 2,000 people. The eruption left a crater 1km wide. At the bottom is a lake, which still bubbles with escaping gas.

LOPSIDED BLAST

Mount St Helens was one of North America's most scenic mountains, with a perfect cone-shaped peak. Then in March 1980, the mountain exploded, and its northern slope collapsed. The eruption left 57 people dead, and threw millions of tonnes of dust into the air.

Peak before

During the blast

Peak after

LAVA ON THE RUN

The world's biggest volcanoes produce runny lava, which pours downhill in red-hot rivers and streams. This kind of lava hardly ever makes volcanoes block up, but it's dangerous because it moves so fast. In 1977, lava surged down the slopes of Nyiragongo, an African volcano, at 60km/h.

STICKY SITUATION

Covered in a heat-resistant suit, a scientist takes a sample of lava from an active volcano. It is dangerous work, particularly in a volcano like this, where the lava is thick and sticky. Instead of flowing away, this kind of lava can block a volcano's vent, making the internal pressure rise until the volcano blasts itself apart. In the explosion, lumps of hot lava – called lava bombs – can be flung 1km through the air.

WEBICORDERS

Days before an eruption, the lava building up under the ground causes small earthquakes, or tremors. Scientists can predict when a volcano is about to explode by picking up these tremors. In the past, the tell-tale quakes were detected with seismograph machines, which showed the wobbling motion of the ground as a graph. Today, we use webicorders, which send out warning information by radio and around the world via the internet.

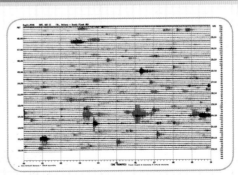

In harm's way

WHEN VOLCANOES ERUPT, all kinds of deadly hazards are suddenly unleashed. Rivers of lava set forests and buildings on fire. Worse still, super-heated clouds of gas and rock can surge down the volcano's sides, smothering anything – and anyone – trying to escape. Meanwhile, volcanic dust reaches high into the atmosphere, where the wind spreads it far and wide.

BURN OUT

On the island of Hawaii, a stream of lava from the Kilauea volcano sets fire to a group of trees. This kind of lava has a temperature of up to 1,000°C – hot enough to set fire to trees and buildings without even touching them. Kilauea's lava often reaches as far as the sea, where it disappears in huge plumes of steam.

spotlight on flying into trouble

On 15 December, 1989, a Boeing 747 flew into a cloud of ash produced by an erupting volcano in Alaska. All four engines shut off, and the plane plunged nearly 4,000m before the pilots managed to get them to restart.

CRUSHED BY ASH

During a big eruption, ash can build up on roads and roofs like a deep layer of snow. However, unlike snow, volcanic ash is heavy – particularly if rain makes it wet. Eventually, the weight can become so great that roofs collapse, killing or injuring people inside. This house was destroyed by ash during the eruption of Tungurahua, a volcano in South America that erupted in 2006.

CLEARING UP

After an eruption is over, the hard work of clearing up begins. These people are sweeping away dust in Quito, the capital of Ecuador, after an eruption 90km away. Volcanic ash is hard and gritty, and it can make car engines seize up. Its one good point is that it is full of minerals, so ash helps to make soil very fertile.

WELL PREPARED

Ordinary dust can make you cough, but breathing volcanic ash can cause bronchitis and other serious diseases. That is because volcanic ash is made of tiny sharp-edged particles of rock and natural glass. It is bad enough if you are healthy, but for people that already have heart or lung problems, it can kill. These children live close to Mount Merapi, the most active volcano in Indonesia. They are well protected against the risks.

The big melt

MANY OF THE WORLD'S HIGHEST VOLCANOES are covered with ice or snow. Around their summits, heat and cold create some of the strangest scenery in the world, including ice towers and steam-filled ice caves. When the volcano erupts, the ice can disappear in minutes as the heat makes it melt. The result is a volcanic flood – one that races downhill, sweeping up mud, ash, whole trees and even boulders the size of cars.

ICE TOWER

Over 3,500m up on Mount Erebus, a tower of ice looms against the bright blue sky. Mount Erebus is in Antarctica, and is the southernmost active volcano in the world. Near its summit, ice towers form where steam comes out of the rock, freezing as it meets the air. The towers grow up to 15m high before their own weight makes them collapse.

! PROTECT YOURSELF

Ash and mudflows are the two biggest dangers in many volcanic eruptions. The best way to protect yourself against ash is to breathe through a piece of cloth. Volcanic floods can strike long after an eruption, so it is important to keep away from low ground.

GLACIER BURST

This bridge was damaged during a huge flood that happened in Iceland in 1996. The flood was triggered by an eruption underneath Iceland's biggest glacier, the Vatnajokull. Water built up under the glacier until finally the ice gave way and a torrent of water was released. At its peak, the flood was 50km wide and up to 5m deep. Fortunately, no one was harmed, but some of Iceland's largest bridges were destroyed as the water poured downhill towards the sea.

FLOODED BY MUD

In 2008, Chile's Chaitén volcano erupted after being silent for nearly 10,000 years. As well as pouring out millions of tonnes of ash, it triggered off volcanic mudflows, known as lahars. Lahars can be extremely dangerous, because they set like concrete when they come to a stop. In the Chaitén eruption, one lahar blocked a river, sending its water straight into a town.

ERUPTIONS are often followed by mud-laden floods

LINGERING DAMAGE

Before Mount Pinatubo erupted in 1991, powerful earthquakes warned that disaster was on its way. About 50,000 people were evacuated before the volcano finally exploded, an operation that saved huge numbers of lives. Since then, many people have moved back to rebuild their homes, but life next to Pinatubo is still not entirely safe. Every year, the rainy season loosens ash on the volcano's slopes, causing dangerous mudslides.

Blasts from the past

THE EARTH IS SCARRED by huge eruptions that happened long ago. Some of them – like the explosion of Krakatoa or Vesuvius – buried ancient towns and cities, and claimed thousands of lives. Much further back in time, ancient eruptions affected prehistoric animals, wiping out entire species by killing off their food. One of the biggest prehistoric eruptions took place in India, more than 60 million years ago. It was so powerful that it may have helped to end the reign of the dinosaurs.

KRAKATOA

The island of Krakatoa blew itself apart in 1883, in an explosion that could be heard over 3,000km away. Up to 30,000 people died in the eruption itself, and in the tsunami that it caused. In 1927, a new volcanic cone emerged from the sea where Krakatoa had once been. It is called Anak Krakatau, or "Child of Krakatoa".

DARK TIMES

The Deccan Plateau, in India, was built up by some of the biggest eruptions the world has ever seen. The eruptions began about 68 million years ago, or 3 million years before the dinosaurs disappeared. Lava from the eruptions formed an immense sheet 2,000m deep, which covered half of the Indian subcontinent. In these hills near the plateau's edge (left), the layers of lava look like dark stripy bands.

spotlight on **year without a summer…**

The summer of 1816 was one of the coldest on record – in North America, rivers were still frozen in July. The culprit was Mount Tambora in south-east Asia. It erupted in 1815, producing so much ash that it blocked out the sun for months.

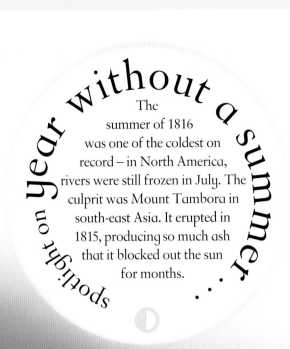

The eruption of KRAKATOA literally *shook* the world

ANCIENT ATLANTIS?

About 3,600 years ago, the Mediterranean island of Santorini exploded, in one of the biggest eruptions of historical times. The centre of the island vanished, leaving a curve of jagged cliffs high over a deep blue bay. Santorini may have inspired the legend of Atlantis, an island civilization that disappeared beneath the waves.

WINDOW ON THE PAST

In 79 AD, the eruption of Mount Vesuvius completely destroyed the Roman city of Pompeii. Blanketed by a deep layer of ash, the city then lay forgotten until it was accidentally rediscovered in 1748. Since then, the ruins of Pompeii have gradually been excavated. Thanks to the ash, they are amazingly well preserved, making Pompeii one of the most fascinating archaeological sites in the world.

Danger zone

WITH ITS SCALDING-HOT SPRINGS and spectacular geysers, Yellowstone National Park has some of the most stunning scenery in North America. But something even more incredible lurks beneath the ground. It is a giant chamber of magma, or molten rock, covered by a lid of solid ground. If the lid melts or cracks – as it has done in the past – the magma will force its way to the surface, and produce an immense explosion. In the last two million years, Yellowstone's magma chamber has exploded three times. The last eruption was about 600,000 years ago, and the next could happen at any time.

GRAND PRISMATIC SPRING

Yellowstone's Grand Prismatic Spring is longer than a football pitch, and nearly 50m deep in the middle. The centre of the spring is too hot for living things, but the shallows near the edge teem with heat-resistant bacteria called thermophiles. These extra-tough microbes can survive temperatures of up to 60°C. They give the spring its extraordinary colours, which slowly change throughout the year.

STEAMING LANDSCAPE

Yellowstone is famous for its wildlife, such as bison, and also for its geysers, which blast steam and boiling water high into the air. One of them, called the Steamboat Geyser, has two openings or vents, like the funnels on a ship. When it erupts, it throws water 100m into the air, making it the tallest geyser in the world. Yellowstone has about 200 active geysers – more than anywhere else on Earth.

EYES ON THE GROUND

Using satellites, scientists can map the ground level at Yellowstone, to see changes caused by volcanic activity. Each map is built up from pictures taken several months apart. The coloured rings show where the ground level has changed. Each complete set of colours marks a fall or rise of nearly 30mm.

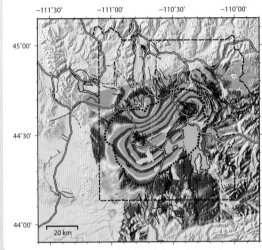

SMOTHERED BY ASH

The last time Yellowstone erupted, most of the western half of the United States was covered by volcanic ash. If the same thing happened today, hundreds of cities would be affected, and tens of millions of people will have to move to safety.

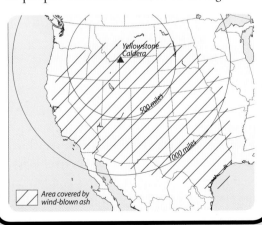

PASSING THROUGH

About 600,000 years ago, Yellowstone was a volcanic wasteland without any signs of life. Today the area is one of North America's busiest national parks, attracting more than two million visitors every year.

19

Life fights back

AFTER AN ERUPTION IS OVER, living things soon start to reclaim the devastated landscape. Insects and birds are often the first to arrive, followed by plants, whose seeds drift through the air. Within a few years, the lava and ash are covered with patches of greenery, as pockets of soil build up, and more plants take root. Decades later, a volcano's slopes are covered with thick forest again, as living things reclaim the ground that they had lost.

GROWING ON LAVA

This plant is sprouting on bare lava on Kilauea – a volcano in the Hawaiian Islands. Lava is hard and unwelcoming, but it does have one big plus: it is full of the minerals that plants need in order to grow. Ferns and shrubs set up home in cracks in the lava and sheltered gulleys. There, the roots are shaded from the sun, and they can collect water when it rains.

Volcanoes HELP life as well as harming it

PLANT PIONEERS

After Mount St Helens erupted in 1980, fireweed, or willowherb (above), was one of the first plants to make a comeback. With its bright red flowers and airborne seeds, it quickly takes over ash-covered ground. The same plant is common in Britain. During World War II, it created a blaze of colour where bombs had scorched the ground.

FUTURE FOREST

When Mount St Helens erupted, millions of trees were destroyed in minutes. The photograph above, taken 15 years later, shows that the forest soon started to grow back. Today, some of these trees are more than 10m high, and will soon be producing seeds themselves. As the forest grows back, it gradually changes, as the first trees to arrive are replaced by taller, slower-growing kinds.

RESTLESS NEIGHBOUR

These ponies are grazing on the slopes of Arenal, an active volcano in Costa Rica, Central America. Like many volcanoes, Arenal is surrounded by rich farmland, because volcanic ash makes for very fertile soil. Arenal was dormant for 400 years, until it came back to life in 1968. Fortunately, its eruptions are only small, so it is not quite as dangerous as it looks.

Spotlight on Surtsey

The island of Surtsey was born in 1963, when it blasted its way through the sea's surface off the coast of Iceland. Since then, scientists have found about 20 kinds of plants on it, together with several species of seabirds.

Earthquakes and landslides

ON 17 JANUARY, 1995, the ground began to shake in the Japanese city of Kobe. In the next 20 seconds, houses collapsed, escaping gas caught fire, and elevated expressways cracked, crashing onto the ground below. It was the most expensive natural disaster on record, and 6,000 people died. Fortunately, earthquakes this big are rare, and many parts of the world never have earthquakes at all. However, like landslides, they can strike at almost any time. If they happen under the ocean floor, the result can be something even more deadly and far-reaching – a tsunami or tidal wave.

Despite being designed to withstand earthquakes, Kobe's roads and railways were badly damaged by the 1995 quake. Here, several pillars of an elevated expressway have given way.

Restless Earth

IN SOME PARTS OF THE WORLD, earthquakes are unknown. In others, the threat of a big quake is never far away. This difference is due to Earth's rocky shell, or crust, which is divided into huge plates that are slowly on the move. The centres of plates are seldom hit by quakes, but if you live near the edge of one, you may be an earthquake expert already. Neighbouring plates often collide or scrape past each other where they meet, triggering huge jolts that make the ground shake.

The next BIG quake, could hit at *any time*

JAGGED EDGE

The San Andreas Fault, in southern California, is one of the most famous earthquake zones in the world. Here, two parts of the Earth's crust are sliding in opposite directions, creating a visible gash 1,200km long. Instead of moving smoothly, the two plates often snag together, creating earthquakes when they separate.

FOLLOWING CLUES

Scientists have discovered that the centre of a quake occurs further along the fault than the last one in the area. Over several decades, quakes travel along the whole fault and then start again at the other end. This is used to predict where and when the next big quake will hit.

spotlight on ups and downs

During an earthquake, the ground can move up and down, as well as from side to side. Sometimes the sea shore is raised by several metres, leaving fish and coral reefs stranded out of the water.

AFTERMATH OF A QUAKE

After the Kobe earthquake hit Japan in 1995, fire burned through many houses in the city, causing as much damage as the earthquake itself. Earthquakes trigger fires by breaking gas pipes and petrol tanks, and by causing sparks. The water supply is often cut, which makes it difficult to put out the fire once it has taken hold.

EARTHQUAKE ZONES

Four-fifths of the biggest earthquakes happen in the "Ring of Fire" – a 40,000km-long zone that surrounds the Pacific Ocean. The Ring of Fire includes the San Andreas Fault, and also the whole of Japan. After this, the second most active earthquake zone runs from southern Europe, through the Himalayas, to Indonesia. In 2004, an earthquake here triggered the Indian Ocean tsunami – one of the deadliest natural disasters ever.

Ring of Fire

Surviving quakes

IN AN EARTHQUAKE, the safest place to be is out of doors. If you are in a car, you may not even notice that a quake is underway. However, if you are in a tall building, even the shudders from small earthquakes are hard to miss, because loose objects rattle around, furniture moves, and overhead lights start to sway. A big earthquake can cause much more serious damage, and your chances of escaping unhurt depend on how you react the moment the earthquake strikes.

QUAKE-PROOF

Some of the world's highest buildings are in earthquake areas. One of the tallest – the Taipei 101 Tower in Taiwan – has a 660-tonne weight on its 88th floor. The weight (below) is hung on 16 cables. If a quake hits, the weight will swing. This absorbs the quake's energy, and stops the tower breaking up.

SEARCHING FOR SURVIVORS

After an earthquake, rescue workers must work fast to pinpoint people trapped in the rubble. It is a race against time because without help, few quake victims survive for more than three days. Specially trained dogs (above) find survivors by smell, while infrared sensors work by detecting people's body heat through the rubble.

Quake-proof buildings *sway* WITHOUT falling apart

EARTHQUAKE DRILL

Every week, millions of people all over the world practise earthquake drill. In cities, buildings empty as warning sirens sound, and people gather at safe assembly areas beyond the reach of falling debris and fires. However, earthquakes often strike suddenly, which can make trying to escape more dangerous than staying inside. When that happens, the first priority is to duck down and get under cover. Here, a Chinese schoolgirl crouches under her desk, using her hands to protect her ears.

PROTECT YOURSELF

Following these simple rules will help you if you are caught up in a quake:

1. Keep calm!

2. If you are indoors, stay indoors – do not waste time trying to get out.

3. Move to a corner away from any windows, and take cover under a sturdy piece of furniture, a table for example.

4. Stay hunched up with your hands over your ears.

5. If you are outside, move away from buildings and any overhead power lines.

6. Remember that lifts and stairs might be damaged in the quake, and aftershocks may hit once the main earthquake is over.

STARTING FROM SCRATCH

The Chinese are used to earthquakes, but they were still caught off guard by a massive jolt that struck the country in May 2008. The quake hit the central province of Sichuan, but it also made buildings shake 1,000km to the east in the port of Shanghai. Altogether, about 70,000 people died, and nearly five million lost their homes.

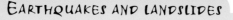
Landslides

GRAVITY IS INVISIBLE, but it has an amazing pulling power. Normally, it keeps things in their place, but sometimes it can tear whole mountain sides apart. If an earthquake or a storm loosens rock or mud, gravity can free it from its moorings, and bring it cascading downhill. Rockslides smash open anything in their way, but mudslides smother buildings like a fast-flowing river, giving little chance of escape.

THE MOUNTAIN THAT FELL APART
In 1903, more than 70 million tonnes of rock crashed down the side of Turtle Mountain in Canada. It was one of the biggest landslides ever recorded, and it left a scar on the mountain that can still be seen (above).

MUDSLIDE IN THE PHILIPPINES
In 2006, mud completely buried the village of Guinsaugon in the Philippines. The village was close to a mountain slope that had been soaked by nearly 200cm of rain in just ten days – as much as London gets in about four months. An earthquake then loosened the mud, and started the deadly slide.

Heavy
RAIN and THICK
mud are a
DEADLY mix

WINCHED TO SAFETY

Landslides are most common in rugged, mountainous areas, and that makes rescue difficult. Helicopter is often the only way to get in fast enough to save lives. Here, a team of rescuers is lowered on to a country road buried by a landslide in northern Japan in 2004. Several cars were buried by the slide after a powerful earthquake had made the hillside unstable a few days before.

HASTY EXIT

Tipped up like cardboard boxes, these houses were caught up in a landslide that hit the Californian coastal town of Laguna Beach in 2005. The landslide struck early in the morning but amazingly no one was killed. Residents had just enough time to scramble outside before their homes slid away.

spotlight on that creeping feeling

Landslides do not always happen quickly. In cold parts of the world, the soil often creeps downhill during the summer, because the surface thaws, but the ground stays frozen deeper down.

Tsunamis

TSUNAMIS ARE THE BIGGEST and most dangerous waves on Earth. Unlike normal waves, most tsunamis are triggered by undersea earthquakes, and this gives them their incredible power. Once a tsunami starts, it spreads across the ocean at up to 1,000km/h, rising up to full height only as it approaches the coast. When the wave hits the shore, a wall of seawater surges far inland, sweeping away almost everything in its path.

GIANT WAVES

Surfers love parts of the world like Hawaii that have giant waves, but the biggest waves ridden by surfers are tiny compared to tsunamis. That is because ocean waves are made by the wind, which usually blows steadily but not very hard. Tsunamis are different; they are formed by a single devastating jolt and move at over half the speed of sound.

LITUYA BAY

The tallest tsunami ever recorded hit Lituya Bay, in Alaska, in 1958. It was 524m high – one and a half times the height of the Eiffel Tower. Unlike most tsunamis, this one was triggered by an earthquake on land, which made millions of tonnes of rock plunge into the sea. The tsunami destroyed forests, harbours and boats (above), but amazingly, only four people died.

DANGER ZONE

Tsunamis are most common around the Indian and Pacific Oceans, because these waters include the Earth's biggest earthquake zones. When a tsunami strikes, the danger is greatest in places closest to the earthquake, particularly where the coast has a lot of bays. Bays work like funnels, piling up the water as it nears the shore. The most tsunami-hit country is Japan: the word "tsunami" was originally Japanese. It means "harbour wave" because the giant waves only rise up when they get near to the shore.

! PROTECT YOURSELF

If you see a sign like this one, you are in a tsunami danger zone. Sensors far out on the seabed detect quakes and raise the alarm. If the alarm sounds, head for high ground – you may have only minutes before the wave arrives.

TSUNAMI
EVACUATION
ROUTE

The Indian Ocean tsunami

ON 26 DECEMBER, 2004, one of the most powerful earthquakes ever recorded struck the seabed off Sumatra, in the eastern Indian Ocean. The jolt created an enormous wave that spread in all directions, like a ripple on a gigantic lake. In the open sea, the tsunami was less than 1m high, but as it reached the coast, it towered up to 25m above the shore. By the time the tsunami had subsided, at least 200,000 people had lost their lives.

SPREADING WAVE

The tsunami took just 15 minutes to reach the nearby coast of Sumatra, catching thousands of people unprepared. It took two hours to reach Thailand and Sri Lanka, and about eight hours to cross the Indian Ocean to hit East Africa. The wave even crossed the Pacific and was seen in Canada and Mexico.

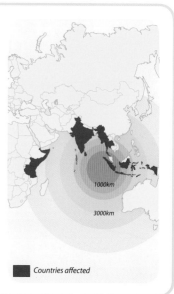

1000km

3000km

■ Countries affected

1 DANGER APPROACHING

These three photographs, taken from a video, show the tsunami hitting the coast of Thailand. Here, the wave already looks gigantic. Its muddy colour comes from sand and grit wrenched from the seabed.

2 BURSTING ASHORE

The giant wave bursts upwards as it hits the top of the beach, beyond the limit of the highest tides. Meanwhile, out to sea, the wave has passed by, and the water looks strangely calm again.

The EARTHQUAKE *moved* over 3 *trillion* TONNES of seawater

WARNING SYSTEM

Since the 2004 tsunami, a warning system has been put in place throughout the Indian Ocean. It uses pressure recorders to detect seabed earthquakes. These flash signals to satellites, warning that a tsunami could be on its way.

3 IMPACT
Seconds later, the full force of the wave hits the trees and buildings on the shore. Unlike a normal wave, this one keeps coming. The water surges far inland before falling back once more.

Extreme storms

REACHING DOWN FROM THE CLOUDS ABOVE, the funnel of a tornado can rip its way through houses and farmland, destroying almost anything in its path. It is an extreme example of a violent disturbance in the atmosphere – in other words, a storm. Storms affect some places more than others, and the damage they can do is colossal. Lightning can set the landscape on fire, thunderstorms can cause flash floods, and a hurricane's strong winds can wreck an entire city as they blow in from the ocean. Immense dust storms and blizzards can bring a whole country to a halt.

Surrounded by a cloud of dust and debris, a tornado skirts close to some houses in the American Midwest. The people in the foreground have just seconds to get out of harm's way.

Hurricanes and typhoons

HURRICANES AND TYPHOONS are the world's largest storms. Both types start far out at sea, and both can cause appalling destruction if they move across land, through wind damage, rain and floods. Hurricane Katrina devastated New Orleans in 2005, but this was small compared to Typhoon Tip, which struck Japan in 1979. It was over 2,000km across.

SPIRAL OF DESTRUCTION

Hurricanes and typhoons have a spiral shape, with bands of storm clouds circulating around a central hole called an eye. The strongest winds blow near the centre of the storm, but the eye itself is eerily calm.

HURRICANE PREDICTION

Hurricanes are easy to track, but even today, scientists cannot predict exactly when and where they will strike land. Instead, weather centres issue hour-by-hour updates of a hurricane's likely path and its strength. A category five hurricane (red, below) – the strongest class – has winds above 250km/h.

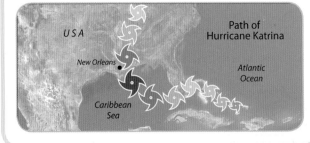

USA

New Orleans

Path of Hurricane Katrina

Atlantic Ocean

Caribbean Sea

Spotlight on America's deadliest hurricane...

In 1900, a hurricane killed up to 12,000 people when it hit Galveston on the coast of Texas. Today, the city is protected by a 5m-high wall that keeps out the sea.

DANGER ZONES

Hurricanes and typhoons need a lot of heat and always start in the tropics. Their names depend on where they start. Hurricanes form in the North Atlantic, but in the North Pacific they are called typhoons. In the Southern Hemisphere the same type of storms are known as tropical cyclones. Hurricanes and typhoons rotate anticlockwise, while tropical cyclones spin in a clockwise direction.

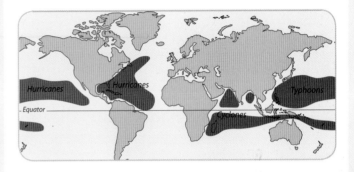

STORM SURGE

As a hurricane nears the coast, it can make the sea pile up into a surge, several metres above its normal level. In 2005, this kind of storm surge caused chaos in New Orleans, as Hurricane Katrina made its way inland. The Mississippi River burst over its banks, or levees, and violent winds ripped houses from their foundations (above). Flooding forced about a million people to leave their homes.

Tornadoes

TORNADOES, OR "TWISTERS", ARE THE MOST violent storms on Earth. Spinning at up to 400km/h, they reach down from the clouds to the ground. After making contact, a tornado wanders about like a living thing, leaving a trail of destruction in its wake. Fortunately, most tornadoes are short-lived. In as little as 30 minutes, the wind starts to slacken, and the tornado finally disappears.

WRECKAGE

Tornadoes happen all over the world, but they are most common in the flat plains of the American Midwest. This wreckage (above) is the centre of Greensburg, Kansas, which was hit by a tornado on 4 May, 2007. The tornado was more than 2.5km wide, and its wind had a top speed of 300km/h. It flattened much of the city, and left 11 people dead.

What is a Tornado?

A tornado is a spinning column of low-pressure air. It is driven by a warm updraught – a strong wind that blows upwards beneath powerful thunderstorms. Most tornadoes are less than 200m across, but the biggest ones on record are over ten times this size.

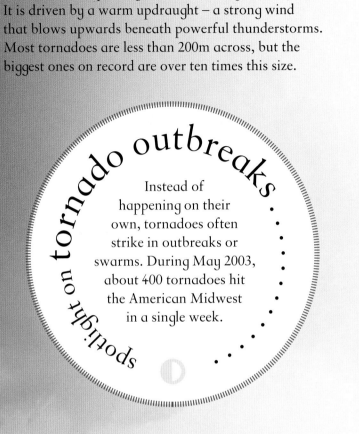

spotlight on tornado outbreaks

Instead of happening on their own, tornadoes often strike in outbreaks or swarms. During May 2003, about 400 tornadoes hit the American Midwest in a single week.

The **United States** has a *thousand* tornadoes a YEAR

Waterspout

Tornadoes don't only happen on land – they can also form over freshwater and the sea. Known as waterspouts, they suck up water from the surface, making a long funnel that reaches up to the clouds. Waterspouts are not as powerful as tornadoes, and they often stay in one place, which makes them easier to avoid. Even so, they are dangerous to swimmers and small boats, and they sometimes sweep fish and other small sea animals high into the air.

Tornado Tracking

Beneath a stormy sky in Oklahoma, a researcher scans the clouds with a Doppler radar. This device works like a police radar, but instead of checking the speed of cars, it looks for fast-moving air currents rushing between the clouds and the ground. These currents show where a tornado is likely to form, and researchers can predict a disastrous tornado in time to issue a warning. Storm research is dangerous work but it has saved many lives.

Dust storms

IN DRY PARTS OF THE WORLD, strong winds can sweep up a huge quantity of dust or sand and carry it into the sky. The result is a sand or dust storm – a thick yellow or orange cloud that blocks out the light from the sun. The cloud forms a menacing wall that can be more than 1km high, and it often seems to roll as it travels across the ground. The storms can cross whole continents or oceans once they are on the move, and the sand and dust piles up on houses, streets and cars when it finally settles back on land.

SAND ON THE MOVE

Seen from space, a 1,000km-long cloud of sand stretches out over the Atlantic Ocean. Sand from the Sahara Desert sometimes reaches the Canary Islands, and it also blows northwards to Europe, before rain washes it out of the air.

spotlight on the dust bowl years

During the 1930s, huge dust storms raged through the American Midwest, when farmland dried up and soil blew away. These "black blizzards" forced about two million people to move home.

TAKING COVER

The West African city of Niamey is near the Sahara Desert, where some of the world's biggest sand storms are born. Here a sand-cloud is approaching the city's outskirts. The normally busy road is empty, as the city's inhabitants take refuge indoors.

HEALTH HAZARD

Shielding their faces, Chinese men battle through a dust storm in the city of Chengdu. Sand and dust feel different, and they do harm in different ways. Sand grains have sharp edges. They can scratch the eyes, and they also get lodged deep inside the ears. Dust particles are usually too small to scratch much, but they are easy to breathe in. If this happens, the body responds by coughing violently – a way of dislodging them before they do any more damage.

DUST PROOF

A camel's nostrils are specially shaped to keep out dust and sand. They are long and narrow, and can close completely in between each breath. Camels also have long eyelashes, which protect their eyes during storms, as well as keeping out the glare of the desert sun.

In 2001,
a cloud of dust from
MONGOLIA
reached the
United States

Lightning

MANY PEOPLE ARE SCARED OF THUNDERSTORMS. While thunder can sound scary, lightning can kill. It happens because electricity gradually builds up in thunderclouds. A lightning bolt suddenly releases this energy, either by jumping to other clouds or to the ground. Lightning bolts last for just a split second, but they can be over 1km long. Every year, more than two thousand people die from being struck by lightning, and many more are injured when it strikes close by.

GATHERING STORM

As lightning flashes on the horizon, these African elephants seem quite unconcerned. Their chances of being hit are small, but even so a few unlucky ones get hit every year. Lightning has even killed an elephant in a circus. The elephant, called Norma Jean, was hit in Illinois in 1972.

MID-AIR STRIKE

Passenger planes usually steer around thunderstorms, because the powerful winds in thunderclouds can cause dangerous turbulence. However, if a plane does find itself in a storm, a lightning strike usually does no damage at all. The reason for this is that a plane's outer body, or fuselage, is made of metal. Metals are good at carrying electric currents, much better than other materials, such as plastics, wood, water, or living bodies. Therefore, the lightning's electricity travels through the fuselage, instead of through the people and sensitive instruments inside.

On average, *passenger planes* get struck by LIGHTNING once a year

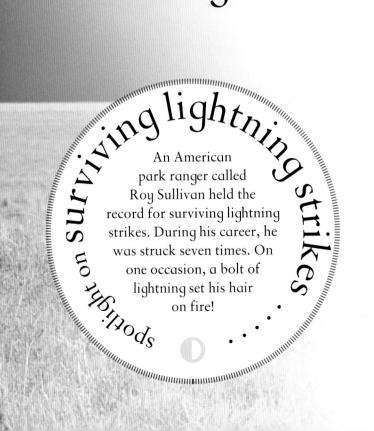

spotlight on surviving lightning strikes

An American park ranger called Roy Sullivan held the record for surviving lightning strikes. During his career, he was struck seven times. On one occasion, a bolt of lightning set his hair on fire!

PROTECT YOURSELF

The best way to protect yourself from lightning is to head indoors. Don't use anything electrical until you are sure that the storm has passed. If you are in a car, stay inside, and don't touch anything made of metal. If you are caught out in the open, stay well away from water, high ground, and most of all from trees.

Snow and ice

Snow is made of ice crystals that form high up in the air. It is legendary for its softness and for the gentle way that it falls. However, on steep mountain sides, snow can be a killer. It can suddenly give way when the weather warms up, ploughing its way downhill. These surges of fallen snow are called avalanches. In an avalanche, more than a million tonnes of snow can be on the move. The snow smashes through trees and houses, setting solid the moment it comes to rest.

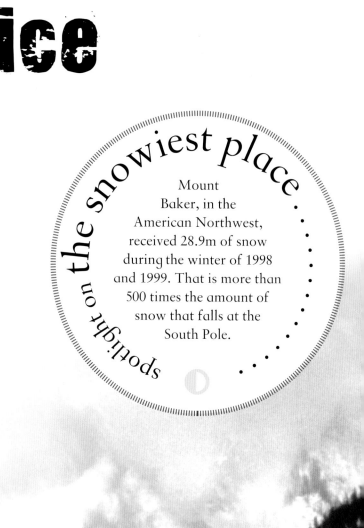

spotlight on the snowiest place

Mount Baker, in the American Northwest, received 28.9m of snow during the winter of 1998 and 1999. That is more than 500 times the amount of snow that falls at the South Pole.

IN THE FIRING LINE

In the United States alone, more than 50 people die in avalanches each year. Most are hit while skiing, but avalanches can also strike people much closer to home. Here, an avalanche surges towards the city of Juneau, in Alaska.

THE GREAT ICE STORM

If the ground is colder than the air higher up, rain sometimes freezes the moment that it lands. Freezing rain is rarer than snow, and it covers everything with a hard layer of ice. In January 1998, up to 10cm of freezing rain fell across eastern Canada and nearby parts of the United States. The sheer weight of ice toppled millions of trees and brought a thousand electricity pylons crashing down.

During an
AVALANCHE,
powdery snow
can move at *over*
250km/h

EMERGENCY ON ICE

Avalanche rescue is a race against the clock, because very few people survive for more than an hour. In the Alps, specially trained dogs locate buried skiers by using their incredibly keen sense of smell. In recent years, rescue efforts have been improved by electronic beacons, which skiers carry with them on the slopes. If a skier is buried, the beacon sends a radio signal through the snow. The rescue team on the surface can pick up the signal, showing them where to dig.

PROTECT YOURSELF

Most fatal avalanches are accidentally triggered by people skiing on unstable snow. To protect yourself, make sure that you always watch out for avalanche warnings. Wear an avalanche rescue beacon and never be tempted to venture off on your own. If you do get caught in moving snow, try to grab a rock or a tree. If you are buried in loose snow, "swim" with your arms to reach the surface.

Heat and drought

LIFE DEPENDS ON WATER, AND THE HOTTER IT GETS, the faster water dries up and disappears. In some parts of the world, it's hot and dry all the time, and the only way to survive is by being well prepared. However, weather patterns change all the time, making it difficult to know where the heat will turn up next. During heatwaves, the thermometer can shoot up to record levels, drying up water supplies, triggering wildfires, and cracking open the ground. Wild plants and animals are built to survive this kind of disaster, but humans begin to struggle when the heat is on.

Shaded by an umbrella, an Indian farmer leads a cow across a barren field. Millions of people like him depend on monsoon rains, which come after months of drought.

Heatwaves

THE HUMAN BODY IS AMAZINGLY GOOD AT coping with extremes. In dry air, people can tolerate temperatures of over 40°C, as long as they have enough to drink. But if the air is hot and humid, the body's natural cooling system starts to break down. The result is heatstroke – a medical emergency that can kill. Most heatstroke victims are caught in the open, in places without water or shade. But during heatwaves, heat can stalk its victims almost anywhere, including homes and city streets.

KILLER HEAT

Shrouded by smog, the city of Paris roasts during the European heatwave of 2003. Across western Europe, temperatures soared to record levels, and the heat was made worse by polluted air. At the time, few people realized how deadly the heat had become, but once the heatwave had finished, European medical records showed that it had claimed 30,000 lives!

spotlight on the world's hottest town

Marble Bar, in Western Australia, has the highest average temperatures of any inhabited place on Earth. In 1923-4, the thermometer stayed above 37°C for 160 days in a row.

STAYING COOL

In deserts, days are hot but nights are often cool. Small mammals – such as this jerboa – beat the heat by coming out when the sun starts to set. In desert countries, humans often behave in the same way.

EARLY BLOOMER

Unlike animals, desert plants can't hide from the glare of the sun. To survive, many of them have water-holding stems, covered with a tough green "skin". This cactus, from America's Mojave Desert, flowers in early spring – one of the few times of the year when it rains.

! PROTECT YOURSELF

In hot dry weather, your body can lose up to 4 litres of water a day in sweat – twice as much as when the weather is cool. To stop yourself dehydrating, you need to drink more than usual, even if you don't feel unusually thirsty. Wear loose-fitting clothing, and stay in the shade as much as you can. If the weather is hot and humid, take things easy, because hard exercise in humid air can make your body rapidly overheat.

SHADY CHARACTER

Desert animals are experts at dealing with extreme heat. This Cape ground squirrel, from Africa's Kalahari Desert, uses its bushy tail as a portable sunshade. When it feeds, it makes sure that its back is facing the sun.

Running dry

Next time you turn on a tap, imagine how you would feel if nothing came out. Surprised, perhaps, and then worried, because water is something that we can't do without. But in many parts of the world, supplies of fresh water are running out. From Arizona to Australia, this slow-motion disaster threatens the way millions of people live.

PULLING THE PLUG

Like a bath that needs cleaning, America's Lake Powell is surrounded by grimy rings. They are left behind by its falling shoreline – the more rings there are, the less water it contains. Lake Powell is one of the biggest reservoirs in the United States. It is fed by snow melting in the Rocky Mountains, but during the last ten years, drought has made it drop to a record low.

MEAGRE HARVEST

After yet another dry year, the wheat in this Australian farm is barely worth harvesting. Since the 1990s, drought has been an almost constant problem in Australia, already the driest continent in the world. To make matters worse, the soil in huge stretches of farmland has become contaminated with salt – a side-effect of clearing the ground to make way for crops.

UNNATURALLY GREEN

Maize is one of the world's thirstiest crops – growing it takes up far more water than people use in their homes. In places with dry climates, this water comes from irrigation. This giant irrigator is on a farm in the American Midwest. Here, water is drawn up from aquifers, layers of water-holding rock under the ground. This underground water is vanishing fast. In 50 years much of it will have run dry.

A MILLION litres of water are needed to produce a TONNE of maize

FILLING UP

Many of the world's poorest farmers live on land that is too dry for raising crops. Instead, they raise animals, taking them to waterholes so that they can drink. Sheep and goats need to drink every day, but camels can go for up to a week without water, as long as they have enough food. They can also drink water that is salty – a big advantage in places where pure water is hard to find.

spotlight on fossil water

The Ogallala Aquifer, in America's Midwest, is one of the world's largest underground water stores. Its "fossil water" formed when glaciers melted at the end of the last ice age, over 10,000 years ago.

Fire!

HEAT AND DROUGHT CREATE IDEAL CONDITIONS for wildfires. In dry parts of the world, fires are a normal part of nature, and the forest eventually grows back. But fires are also started deliberately – either by people looking for excitement or by farmers wanting to clear the ground. Today, the largest wildfires are in the tropics. There, huge areas of rainforest have been burned by people who need land.

DEADLY BLAZE

Some forest fires stay close to the ground, where they burn away bushes and fallen wood. A crown fire is different, and much more dangerous. It sets entire trees alight, from the ground right up to the tips of their highest branches. Crown fires are so hot that they suck air towards them, making forests burn even more fiercely. When people are trapped by crown fires, their chances of escape are very small.

spotlight on deadly wildfire

In January 1939, one of the world's worst ever bushfires burned 20,000sq km of forest and scrub in Victoria, Australia. Triggered by lightning during a heatwave, the fires killed more than 70 people.

WATER BOMB

Swooping down close to the flames, a helicopter drops water on a fire on the U.S.-Mexico border. Helicopters are often used to fight fires in remote places, and ones where water is hard to find. As well as dropping water, they can spray fires with fire-retardants – chemicals that help to quench the flames. Some fire-retardants work like fertilizers, helping a burned forest to grow back again.

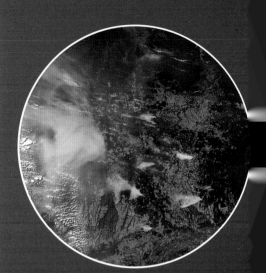

UP IN SMOKE

Seen from space, clouds of smoke drift over southern Brazil, showing where the Amazon rainforest is on fire. Over the last 20 years, nearly a fifth of the Amazon has been burned to make way for farms. In the damp climate, trees can smoulder for months, and the ground is left covered with charred stumps.

FIRE DOWN BELOW

In 1962, a coal mine caught fire underneath the town of Centralia in Pennsylvania. The fire has been burning ever since, and the town has been abandoned to its fate. The air smells of smoke, steam pours out of cracks in the roads, and snow melts as soon as it hits the ground.

Surviving the flames

IF YOU'RE THREATENED BY A WILDFIRE, the first thing you need to do is get safely away from the flames. But in nature, trees and other plants can't pull up their roots and run. Instead, some of them have built-in fire-resistance, and soon start re-sprouting once a fire has passed. Animals usually run or fly for their lives, but some are attracted by fire, because it gives them a chance of finding food.

FIGHTING FIRE WITH FIRE
It sounds strange, but one of the best ways of stopping a fire is to start smaller fires downwind. These "controlled burns" clear away dead brush, which means that there is no fuel for the wildfire to burn.

SMOKY-FLAVOURED FOOD
These white storks have been attracted by a grassfire on the African plains. Standing close to the flames, they snap up grasshoppers, lizards and other small animals trying to escape from the heat. The storks fly high up, so they can see the smoke from far away.

BURSTING INTO GROWTH

Australian plants are experts at surviving wildfires. After being burned right down to the ground, these grass trees are starting to grow new bright green leaves. The charred trees in the background are also still alive, but will take longer to sprout.

Some plants NEED FIRE to release *their seeds*

GIANT WOOD WASP

When a fire is safely out, some insects fly in to lay their eggs on the charred trees. Many of them use the chemicals in smoke to guide them to their target. These insects include wood-boring beetles, and also black and yellow wood wasps. This female wood wasp has a long egg-laying tube that bores into charred branches. Her eggs hatch into grubs that feed on the wood.

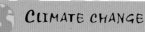

climate change

If you've ever been caught in extreme weather, it's not something that you'll forget quickly. The world's climate is quite different. You can't experience it directly, because it is made up of weather patterns all over the globe. The climate is always changing, but instead of taking hours or days, like weather, some of these changes can take a century or more. Today, the world's climate is warming up, and it is almost certain that humans are at least partly to blame. A warmer climate may sound like good news, but it could be one of the worst disasters that humans have ever had to face.

In recent years, the Arctic's sea ice has been melting fast. If it continues at this rate, the Arctic Ocean will be entirely ice-free during summer by 2030, and many shoreline glaciers will have disappeared.

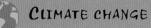
Global warming

GLOBAL WARMING IS A HOT TOPIC in more ways than one. Not everyone believes that it's happening, or that humans are to blame. But nearly all scientists do, and they think it could cause lasting damage to the environment, and wipe out all kinds of living things. Unlike other disasters, this one has happened because we have changed the atmosphere by burning fossil fuels. To reduce global warming, we will have to make big changes to the way we live.

UP IN SMOKE

This coal-burning power station in Arizona is just one of tens of thousands all over the world. The Earth has huge reserves of coal, and it is used to generate nearly half our electricity. The bad news is that burning coal makes global warming worse.

Greenhouse gases trap escaping heat, keeping the Earth warm

Atmosphere

The Earth reflects some sunlight back into the air as heat

THE GREENHOUSE EFFECT

If you've heard about global warming, the chances are that you've also heard about the greenhouse effect. Are they the same thing? The answer is no. The greenhouse effect is a natural feature of the atmosphere, produced by gases such as carbon dioxide, or CO_2. "Greenhouse gases" trap some of the Sun's heat, keeping the Earth comfortably warm. But by burning coal, oil and gas, we have increased the level of carbon dioxide, making the greenhouse effect stronger. As a result, the Earth is warming up even more.

CRUNCH TIME

Today, there are over 600 million cars in the world – or about one for every ten people on the planet. Practically all of them run on oil, and so do all the world's trucks, ships and planes. Every single drop of that oil adds to global warming, because it releases carbon dioxide when it is burned. With the planet warming up, we need to find alternative fuels, and fast.

Global warming could make DESERTS and DISEASES spread

DAMAGED REPUTATION

Nuclear power can help fight global warming, because it produces electricity without releasing CO_2. However, many people think that it is too dangerous, after a disastrous accident at the Chernobyl nuclear plant in 1986 (above).

RENEWABLE ENERGY

With their sails spinning in the breeze, a dozen wind turbines can generate enough electricity to power a small town. This kind of energy is renewable – in other words, it won't ever run out, unlike energy from coal or oil. Renewable energy can be collected from many sources, including sunlight, water, waves and the tides, and it is clean and safe. It also has another big advantage: it does not add to global warming because it doesn't involve burning fuels.

Patterns from the past

It's hard to predict the Earth's future climate, but much easier to look back into the past. All over the Earth, from deserts to the poles, scientists have found that the climate never stays the same for long. Some of these changes take thousands or millions of years, but others are much faster. These rapid changes are the most serious, because they can make it hard for people to survive.

EVIDENCE IN ROCK
These prehistoric rock paintings come from Tassili N'Ajjer, in the heart of the Sahara Desert. They are over 6,000 years old, and they show that the Sahara was once a fertile land, full of wildlife.

FROM GRASSLAND TO DESERT
Today, Tassili N'Ajjer is dry and windswept, and its animal herds are long gone. Hardly anybody lives here, because the climate has become so dry. There is no soil, and whole years can go by without any rain.

FROZEN OUT

These ruins are at Brattahlid in Greenland – a settlement founded by the Vikings nearly a thousand years ago. When the Vikings discovered Greenland, the world climate was warming up. They started farming on Greenland's ice-free southern coast, and lived in houses built of stone. At first, the settlement prospered, but slowly their luck began to change. Over the next 300 years, the cold gradually returned, and the Vikings were unable to grow enough food. After a long struggle against hunger, Greenland's Vikings finally died out.

250 million years ago, ANTARCTICA *had a subtropical climate*

PLANTS FROM THE POLES

This fossil fern comes from Antarctica – the coldest continent on Earth. It dates back millions of years, to a time when Antarctica was much farther north than it is today. Its climate was warm enough for plants, and it even had its own dinosaurs. All of them slowly died out when Antarctica shifted southwards, and became covered by ice.

SECRETS INSIDE ICE

The world's ice sheets are made of compressed snow, which has built up over millions of years. By sampling the ice, scientists can build up a climate record stretching far back into the past. Some samples are taken at the surface, but others are collected by hollow drills that reach down 2km or more. These deep samples include bubbles of ancient air – something that is extremely useful for scientists studying the greenhouse effect.

ice ages

TODAY, THE WORLD IS WARMING UP, and many of the world's glaciers are shrinking fast. But about 18,000 years ago, during the last ice age, exactly the opposite was happening. Ice covered all of northern Europe and a large part of North America, and as it spread southwards, it bulldozed the ground, crushing everything in its path. This ice age wasn't the first the world has seen, and it is unlikely to be the last.

THE ICE EDGE

Seen from the air, the edge of the Greenland ice sheet looks like a gigantic crumpled blanket. During the last ice age, scenery like this could be seen right across the northern hemisphere. Ice covered nearly a third of the planet, compared to about a tenth today.

spotlight on the big freeze

There have been four major ice ages in the history of the Earth. During the coldest, about 700 million years ago, ice covered most of the land on the planet.

ARCTIC TUNDRA

Until about 12,000 years ago, the ice-free parts of Europe and North America were covered mainly by tundra – a cold, windswept landscape scattered with small trees. Despite its harsh climate, the tundra was home to spectacular ice age mammals, including woolly mammoths and woolly rhinoceroses. These massive plant-eaters were well protected against the cold, but they gradually died out as the ice age ended and the climate warmed. The last woolly mammoths lived on Wrangel Island in the Arctic Ocean. They died out less than 4,000 years ago.

LEFT BEHIND

Ice age glaciers often gouged out huge boulders, and carried them far away. When the ice melted, the boulders were left behind. This one, in California's Yosemite Valley, is as high as a single storey house. The world's largest boulder, in Canada, is 40m long, and weighs 16,500 tonnes.

GLACIERS IN THE LAST ICE AGE

This map shows the furthest spread of the ice about 18,000 years ago. North America was covered as far south as present-day New York, and in Europe, the ice reached southern England. Then, about 12,000 years ago, the climate began to warm, and the ice started to retreat. Scientists think that ice ages are caused by a number of things, including variations in the Earth's orbit around the Sun.

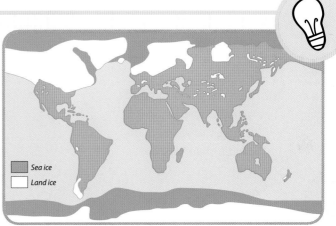

Sea ice

Land ice

shifting shores

THE SEA IS A DANGEROUS NEIGHBOUR, particularly when the wind whips it up during storms. Over the centuries, the sea has broken through countless flood defences and claimed many lives. Keeping it back is hard but it is made harder still because the ocean is on the rise. Since the end of the last ice age, melting glaciers have poured water into the oceans, lifting them by the height of a ten-storey building. Today, the rise is speeding up, threatening millions of people who live on low-lying coasts.

DICING WITH DEATH

Giant breakers smash into the sea wall at Kalk Bay – a fishing port in South Africa. The bay is famous for its huge, rogue waves, which appear without warning and sweep people into the sea. Luckily, these sightseers survived.

spotlight on the expanding seas

Melting ice isn't the only thing that makes the sea level rise. If the climate gets warmer, seawater expands. This process is slow. It takes centuries to start, and even longer to stop.

ISLANDS AT RISK

The Maldives Islands, in the Indian Ocean, are the lowest-lying country in the world. Perched on ancient coral reefs, they have just a few centimetres of soil, and their highest point is less than 2.5m above the sea. More than 300,000 people live on the islands, and for them, sea level rise is a deadly serious matter. If it continues for much longer, the Maldives could be swamped, forcing the entire population to move elsewhere.

In 2100, THE SEA

could be nearly a *metre higher* than today

DOUBLE TROUBLE

Bangladesh is one of the world's poorest countries, and also has the greatest risk of floods. During the monsoon season, its rivers burst their banks, while huge storms drive the sea far inland. These Bangladeshi children (above) are using a well that has been sandbagged against the floods, helping to keep its water clean.

ON THE EDGE

After a stormy winter in 1998, these houses in California were left teetering on the edge of a cliff. One even had its living room sawn off so that it would not drag the rest of the house over the edge. Scenes like these could become more common in the future, because the sea will become stormier as the world warms up.

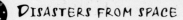

Disasters from space

MOST DISASTERS START RIGHT HERE ON EARTH. However, our world faces even bigger threats lurking in the vastness of space. Instead of being empty, space is full of objects moving at incredible speeds. Some are little bigger than specks of dust, but others – called asteroids – can weigh millions of tonnes. If one of these giant rocks collides with the Earth, the result could be more devastating than all the world's atomic bombs exploding at the same time. Fortunately, the chances of this happening are tiny, but the risk is still there. The last time it happened was millions of years ago, but no one knows when an asteroid will strike again.

If a giant asteroid was pulled off course by our planet's gravity, it might hit Earth with enormous force. The impact would vaporize most of the asteroid and throw an immense cloud of ash and rock into the atmosphere. The rocks would rain down across Earth starting enormous fires. Once the fires had died down, the dust cloud would block out the Sun's heat, creating a cold winter that would last for years.

Out of the unknown

In January 1801, an Italian astronomer noticed a tiny point of light between the planets Mars and Jupiter. He had discovered Ceres – the first known asteroid, and the largest. Since then, thousands more asteroids have been discovered, all orbiting around the Sun. Most asteroids stay in their orbit, which keeps them safely out of harm's way, but every year, a small number get pulled off course. These are the ones that matter most, because they might end up on a collision course with the Earth.

THE ASTEROID BELT

Shaped like a gigantic ring, the asteroid belt is the most crowded part of the Solar System. A few asteroids are like miniature planets, but most are boulders less than a metre across. There are so many asteroids that they sometimes collide with each other as they move around the Sun. When this happens, fragments can be knocked off course, turning into meteorites that head towards the Earth.

Spotlight on fiery comets

Comets contain ice and dust as well as rock. They develop bright tails when they come close to the Sun, and then fade away as they loop back into deep space.

A LANDING ON EROS

In 2001, a space probe landed on Eros, one of the largest asteroids that orbits close to the Earth. Eros is 33km long, and has a slender "waist" that you could walk around in less than two hours. Despite being tiny compared with planets, an object this size would cause catastrophic damage if it ever moved out of its orbit and hit the Earth. Fortunately, it has a long record of being well behaved.

© Detlev van Ravenswaay

The largest known comet is 40km wide

RIGHT ON TIME

Unlike asteroids, comets follow a lot of different timetables as they move around the Sun. One of the best known, called Halley's Comet, returns every 75 years. It is due next in 2061. At the other extreme, Comet Hale-Bopp has much further to travel. It last appeared in 1997, and won't be back again until the year 4380!

MYSTERY IN SIBERIA

In June 1908, a huge explosion rocked the Tunguska River region – a remote part of Siberia. Eyewitnesses reported seeing a fireball in the sky, and over 3,000 sq km of forest were flattened, with all the trees pointing away from the blast. Scientists think that the explosion was caused by a large meteorite breaking up in mid-air.

Target Earth

EARTH HAS A LONG HISTORY OF BEING BOMBARDED from outer space. Every year, thousands of meteorites streak through its atmosphere, burning up long before they hit the ground. However, just occasionally, something really big heads our way, and punches a giant crater in the Earth's surface. These craters are scattered all over the world, but they are not always easy to find. Some have only been discovered in recent years, thanks to satellites that spot them from far above the ground.

GREAT BALL OF FIRE

The Barringer Meteor Crater, in Arizona, is more than 1km across and nearly 200m deep. It was formed about 50,000 years ago by a meteorite weighing more than 100,000 tonnes. When the meteorite hit the ground, it would have been travelling at about 45,000 km/h – fast enough to vaporize in a ball of fire while the crater was being formed.

TELL-TALE RING

Manicouagan Crater, in eastern Canada, was made by an asteroid measuring 5km across that hit the Earth 200 million years ago. Today the crater is used as a ring-shaped reservoir, which makes it easy to see from the air. The impact was so powerful that the crater took about a thousand years to cool down.

spotlight on a direct hit

In 1954, American Anne Hodges became the only person ever known to have been struck by a meteorite. She was hit while sleeping, and escaped with no more than a severe bruise on her hip.

MOON CRATERS

Unlike the Earth, the Moon's surface is not smoothed away by the wind and rain. Many of its craters have existed for billions of years, and the biggest often have smaller craters inside them. The largest crater of all is near the Moon's south pole. It measures an incredible 2,300km across – over half as wide as the Moon itself. It was probably caused by a sideways impact, instead of one that hit the Moon head-on.

The
LARGEST
known crater
on Earth is
over 300km
across

METEORITES FROM MARS

A few of the meteorites that fall to Earth originally came from Mars. This one was spotted on Antarctica's ice cap – a great place for meteorite-hunting because dark objects stand out against the pale ice. Martian meteorites interest scientists, because they contain some of the same chemicals found in Earth's living things.

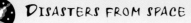

The end of the dinosaurs

ABOUT 65 MILLION YEARS AGO, something astounding happened to life on Earth. The dinosaurs abruptly disappeared. Along with them went many other kinds of animals, including flying reptiles, or pterosaurs, and reptiles called plesiosaurs that lived in the oceans. Plant life was also devastated, as gigantic fires swept across the Earth's surface. This disaster may have had several causes, but the biggest was almost certainly a massive meteorite from space.

HORIZON ON FIRE

With fire on the horizon, a herd of plant-eating titanosaurs try to escape. These giant dinosaurs would have died soon after the meteorite strike, because their food would have vanished within weeks.

Spotlight on mass extinctions

There have been at least five mass extinctions during the history of life on Earth. The biggest, about 250 million years ago, killed off nearly three-quarters of all the animals on land.

WINNERS AND LOSERS

Pterosaurs were the biggest flying animals the world has ever seen. They ruled the skies for millions of years, but died out after the meteorite strike. However, flying animals did not all vanish. Insects survived, and so did birds. The first birds evolved from dinosaurs, and their descendants are still with us to this day.

FINAL FLOURISH

The Age of the Dinosaurs lasted over 150 million years, and many of the biggest kinds died out long before it finished. However, one of the best known, Tyrannosaurus rex, was alive right until the end. Experts are not sure whether it used its huge teeth for hunting, or for ripping up dead remains, but it depended on plant-eating dinosaurs for its food. When they died out, it did as well.

GRAVITY MAP

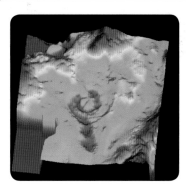

- ● *high-density rocks*
- ● *low-density rocks*
- ● *normal-density rocks*

This map shows the seafloor off Mexico's Yucatan Peninsula – where the meteorite is thought to have landed, bringing the Age of the Dinosaurs to an end. The map was made by sensing variations in gravity. It shows a circular crater, 160km across. The middle has low-density rocks while the rim is made of high-density rocks. This arrangement is the result of rock being blasted out from the centre during the impact.

CHAIN OF DISASTERS

Some scientists think that the dinosaurs were killed off by a series of disasters, instead of a single one. Volcanic eruptions might have filled the atmosphere with smoke, dimming the sun and making it harder for plants to grow. With fewer plants, there would have been less food. Meanwhile, the sea level fell, drying out shallow coasts and coral reefs. This change could explain why plesiosaurs and many other marine animals also disappeared.

Heading off disaster

IT'S A SCARY THOUGHT: somewhere out in the Solar System, a giant meteorite could be heading our way. Until recently, scientists had no way of detecting this danger until it was far too late to respond. However, thanks to better telescopes, we can spot incoming objects while they are still deep in space, and our chances of heading off a deadly collision are improving all the time.

SEARCHING THE SKIES

The Arecibo radio telescope, in Puerto Rico, is the biggest of its kind in the world. It has a collecting dish over 300m across, built into a natural hollow in the ground. Instead of gathering light, it searches the sky using radio waves. Telescopes like this can pinpoint asteroids millions of miles away, while they are still several years' journey from the Earth.

Over 5,000 potentially DANGEROUS asteroids

Spotlight on a date for your diary

In 2029, the asteroid Apophis will speed past the Earth, coming closer than many orbiting satellites. Apophis is about 200m long, and weighs nearly 3 million tonnes!

KEEPING TRACK

Orbiting telescopes give an even better view of asteroids deep in space. Once an asteroid has been spotted, its path can be calculated, to see if there is any danger of it coming close to Earth. The most dangerous objects are ones more than 100m across, which come within 10 million km of Earth's own orbit.

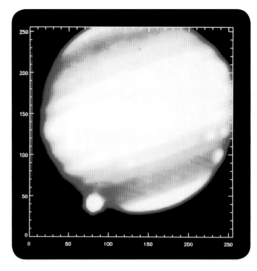

CRASH LANDING

In 1994, astronomers got a first-hand view of a collision in space. After swerving close to Jupiter, comet Shoemaker-Levy broke into more than 20 pieces, which plunged into the giant planet's surface. This photograph shows the aftermath of the collision – the bright orange spots at the bottom are places where the comet hit.

are currently being tracked

Glossary

Active volcano A volcano that is erupting, or likely to erupt at any time.

Aquifer A natural store of water beneath the surface of the ground. In an aquifer, the water fills small spaces inside layers of rock.

Asteroid A rocky object that is smaller than a planet but bigger than a meteor. Most asteroids orbit the Sun between Mars and Jupiter.

Climate The pattern of weather in any place, or across the whole of the Earth.

Climate change Any lasting change in overall weather patterns. When people talk about climate change, they usually mean across the whole of the Earth.

Comet A lump of ice and rock that develops a long "tail" when it orbits close to the Sun. The tail is made of dust and gas. It points away from the Sun, and gradually fades away as the comet heads back into space.

Controlled burn Stopping a wildfire by setting off small fires downwind. Once the small fires have died down, the wildfire has nothing left to burn.

Crater A circular hollow in the ground, often with a raised edge. Craters are made by volcanic eruptions, and also by meteorites hitting the ground from space.

Crown fire The hottest kind of forest fire. Instead of burning off dead branches on the ground, it reaches right up into the crowns of living trees.

Crust The outer layer of the Earth. The crust is made of solid rock, and it forms the continents and the seabed.

Cyclone A giant area of low pressure in the atmosphere. Cyclones are easy to see from space because they are surrounded by a spiral of clouds. In warm parts of the world, tropical cyclones can develop into violent storms known as hurricanes and typhoons.

Dehydration Running out of water. During heatwaves, dehydration can be fatal.

Dormant volcano A volcano that has not erupted for hundreds of years. Dormant volcanoes can still be dangerous, because they may become active again without warning.

Earth tremor A mini-earthquake. Earth tremors are common just before major quakes, and also after them.

Electricity A flow of electrons that runs through a material. Electricity can move through almost anything but it is carried best by metals.

Eruption A volcanic explosion. During an eruption, molten rock, or magma, rises to the surface and then pours out as lava. Exploding gas can also hurl ash high into the sky.

Extinct volcano A volcano that has stopped erupting. The world has far more extinct volcanoes than active ones.

Fault A line where two blocks of rock have slipped past each other.

Fossil Remains of living things that have been preserved in rock.

Fossil fuel A fuel made from the buried remains of living things. Fossil fuels include coal, oil and natural gas, and they take millions of years to form.

Fossil water Water that has been stored in an aquifer for thousands of years.

Geyser A place where jets of boiling water and steam erupt out of cracks in the ground.

Global warming A rise in the Earth's surface temperature. Global warming can be caused by many different things. One of the most important is an increase in the greenhouse effect.

Greenhouse effect A natural process that helps to keep the Earth warm. It makes the atmosphere work like a greenhouse, trapping the Sun's heat.

Greenhouse gas A gas in the atmosphere that helps the Earth to trap heat. The most important greenhouse gases are water vapour and carbon dioxide.

Humidity The level of water vapour in the atmosphere. Unlike clouds, water vapour is invisible.

Hurricane A violent tropical storm in the northwest Atlantic. Hurricanes form out to sea, and often hit land in the Caribbean and south-eastern United States.

Ice ages Times in the Earth's history when the planet was much colder than today. The last ice age lasted about 2 million years, and ended 10,000 years ago.

Ice core A long cylinder of ice collected by drilling down into an ice sheet. Ice cores help scientists to find out about the climate long ago.

Ice storm A storm of rain that freezes the moment it lands. During an ice storm, rain falls through a layer of cold air just above the ground. The cold air chills the raindrops, and they freeze the moment they touch anything solid.

Lahar A mudflow that follows a volcanic eruption. Lahars happen when snowfields or glaciers suddenly melt, sweeping mud and ash downhill.

Lava Red-hot molten rock or magma that pours out of a volcano. In some volcanoes, it flows many kilometres before it finally cools and sets solid.

Mass extinction The disappearance of lots of different living things, at roughly the same time. Fossils show that mass extinctions have occurred several times during the past. After each mass extinction, life has taken millions of years to recover.

Meteorite A rocky or metallic object that has hit the Earth from space. Only the biggest meteorites survive their fall through the atmosphere. Small ones burn up, turning into shooting stars.

Microbes Living things that can be seen only with the help of a microscope.

Minerals Natural chemicals that make up lava and solid rocks.

Plate One of the huge pieces that makes up the Earth's crust. There are nine large plates and lots of smaller ones, and they are all slowly on the move. Most of the Earth's volcanoes and earthquake zones are in places where plates meet or spread apart.

Renewable energy Energy that cannot run out, unlike energy from fossil fuels. Renewable energy sources include sunshine, running water and the wind.

Smog A kind of air pollution caused by factory chimneys and car exhausts. Smog is often worse in sunny weather, because sunshine makes polluting chemicals react with each other.

Storm surge Dangerously high sea levels that happen during a storm. In a hurricane, storm surges can raise the water level by as much as 5m – enough to cause flooding far inland.

Tidal wave Another name for a tsunami.

Tornado A small but extremely powerful column of spiralling air. As the wind rushes around the column, it sucks up all kinds of objects, including roofs and even cars.

Tropical rainforest A kind of forest that grows near the equator, where the climate is warm and wet all year round. Tropical rainforests have a large share of the world's wildlife, but they are disappearing fast.

Tundra A cold and mainly treeless landscape in the far north. Tundra plants and animals have to survive winters up to nine months long.

Typhoon A name used for tropical storms in the north-western Pacific region. These are the most powerful storms in the world.

Waterspout A tornado that forms over water.

Index

Acknowledgements

The publishers would like to thank the following for permission to use their material. Every care has been taken to trace copyright holders. However, if there have been unintentional omissions or failure to trace copyright holders, we apologise, and will, if informed, endeavour to make corrections in any future edition.

KEY
t = top; c = centre; b = bottom; r = right; l = left

Ardea 41cl (Pat Morris); 55tl (Jean Paul Ferrero)

Corbis 8-9 (© Alberto Garcia); 13b (© WEDA/epa); 15tl (© Reuters); 18b (© W. Perry Conway); 21 (© Robert Harding/Robert Harding World Imagery); 22-23 (© TWPhoto); 24 (© Tom Bean); 26bc (© Simon Kwong/Reuters); 33t (© Dadang Tri/Reuters); 52-53 (© Ted Soqui); 55cr (© Ariel Skelley); 58-59 (© Momatiuk-Eastcott); 60b (© Sebastien Cailleux); 63c (© David Muench)

Cosmographics 19br (based on Figure 3.2 (p.49) from Windows into the Earth: The Geologic Story of Yellowstone and Grand Teton National Park, by Robert B. Smith & Lee J. Siegel, published by Oxford University Press, 2000, (adapted from A.M. Sarna-Wojcicki and J. O. Davis: Quaternary Tephrochronology/ Quarternary Nonglacial Geology: Conterminous U.S., The Geology of North America. K-2: 93-1 16, 1991); 25 br; 32 tr; 63 br

FLPA 30b (Steve McCutcheon); 39t (H. Hoflinger); 43b (Ray Bird); 65tl (Wolfgang Herath/Imagebroker)

Getty Images 28-29; 40-41 (AFP); 45t (AFP); 48-49 (AFP); 50tr (AFP); 61t (National Geographic)

Olivier Grunewald 2-3

Gary Hebert 29tl

mikereyfman.com 50b

NASA 36-37 (GSFC/Jacques Descloitres, MODIS Rapid Response Team); 68-69 (JPL-Caltech/T. Pyle [SSC]); 75tl

National Geographic Images 10-11 (Carsten Peter)

Nature Picture Library 49 (Hermann Brehm); 51b (Doug Allen)

PA Photos 4-5 (Pavel Rahman/AP); 32 (both), 32b-33b (AP); 29b (Nick Ut/AP); 46-47 (Gaurav Tiwari/AP); 59tr (STR/AP)

Photolibrary 43t (Simonsen Simonsen)

Photoshot 55bl (Stephen Dalton/NHPA); 73br (Stephen Krasemann/NHPA)

Reuters 1 (Jo Yong hak); 6-7 (Arko Datta); 15cr (Stringer Chile); 16-17 (Supri Supri); 25 (Kimimasa Mayama); 26tr (Tony Gentile); 27t (Jo Yong hak); 27b (David Gray); 29tr (Kimimasa Mayama); 41t (China Photos); 45cl (Michaela Rehle); 53b (Lucas Jackson); 64-65 (Philip Massie); 65cr (Rafiquar Rahman); 65b (Sean Ramsey)

Rex Features 15bl (Sipa Press); 26bl (Action Press); 31r; 44 (NBCUPhotobank)

Science Photo Library 10c; 12-13, 13t (Stephen & Donna O'Meara); 13c (Dr Morley Read); 14–15 (George Steinmetz); 30-31 (G. Brad Lewis); 32-33 background (Royal Astronomical Society); 34-35 (Mike Agliolo); 38-39 (Reed Timmer); 38l (Mike Theiss); 39b (Jim Reed); 40tr (M-SAT Ltd); 42-43 (Adam Jones); 49tl (E.R. Degginger); 53t (NASA); 54t (Kari Greer); 56-57 (Louise Murray); 60tr (George Holton); 61c (British Antarctic Survey); 61b (Louise Murray); 62-63 (Bernhard Edmaier); 66-67 (Richard Bizley); 69tl (Detlev van Ravenswaay); 69cr (RIA Novosti); 70-71 (Tony Craddock); 70tr (Planetobserver); 71br (NASA); 72-73 (Mark Garlick); 72t-73t (Joe Tucciarone); 73tr (Mark Pilkington/Geological Survey of Canada); 73bl (Stephen & Donna O'Meara); 74-75 (David Parker); 75tr (California Association for Research in Astronomy)

Shutterstock 11tr (Jack Haefner); 17t (Petros Tsonis); 17b (Kevin Lings); 18-19 (Katrina Leigh); 19bl (Jerry Sharp); 20tr (Nathan Jaskowiak; 31bl (Michael Ledray); 37b (Brian Nolan); 49cl (Mike Brake); 51t (Stacey Lynn Brown); 59tl (egd); 59br (MaxFX); 63t (FloridaStock) ; 71tr (David W. Kelley)

Still Pictures 54b (Michel & Christine Denis-Huot/BIOS)

The Pacific Northwest Seismic Network, University of Washington 11br

Topfoto 16b (Dinodia)

U.S. Forest Service, Mt St Helens National Volcanic Monument 10bl (Jim Nieland)

USGS 10bc (Austin Post); 10br (Lyn Topinka); 20bl (Lyn Topinka); 20br

C. Wicks, U.S. Geological Survey, Yellowstone Volcano Observatory 19tr

Colin Woodman 58 bl

Useful websites

US Geological Service Volcano Movies
http://hvo.wr.usgs.gov/gallery/kilauea/volcanomovies/
Time-lapse movies of the world's most active volcanoes in the Hawaiian Islands. Includes pictures of lava fountains and lava pouring into the sea.

Savage Earth: Earthquakes
http://www.pbs.org/wnet/savageearth/earthquakes/index.html
Lots of facts about earthquakes, including animations showing how different kinds of seismic waves travel through the ground.

National Hurricane Center
http://www.nhc.noaa.gov/
Run by the US National Weather Service, this information-packed website contains alerts and satellite pictures of hurricanes as they develop. In the North Atlantic, the hurricane season normally runs from June to the end of November.

NASA Near Earth Object Program
http://neo.jpl.nasa.gov/images/
This NASA website contains a host of pictures and animations of asteroids, meteorites and comets. They include pictures of comet Shoemaker-Levy as it hit the surface of Jupiter.